... three little friends who want to be friends with you. If you let them, they'll take you on the most magical adventures you can imagine.

Who are they? Their names are Heada, Heartly and Doofer. They're all very different, because they come from three different lands in the wonderful Kingdom of Theysay.

This is Heada  from The Land of Thinking. She wears big, green glasses and, like all the Thinkers, she's a whiz at thinking. Quick as a wink she can think up an answer, make up a rainy day game or find a hiding place.

This is Heartly from The Land of Feeling. He has long, floppy ears and soft, cuddly fur. Like everyone in his land, Heartly feels a million emotions. In a second, his feelings can change from sad to happy, or from scared to excited.

This is Doofer from The Land of Doing. He's always ready for action. He can build a birdhouse, hit a homerun or juggle three oranges in one hand! When he's busy (which is constantly!), he's a buzzing whirlwind with long, yellow hair flying in the breeze.

In the Kingdom of Theysay also lives a mysterious and magical man known as The Great Theysayer. His home is the Hall of Harmoniousness, which stands high on a majestic mountain.

They say The Great Theysayer is very wise. Over the years, he has learned the truths about all the "they says" that have ever been said.

One day he looked at the many books of "they says" in his library and remembered how long and hard he had worked to become so wise. Wouldn't it be wonderful, he thought, if children could learn more easily! But how?

Gradually a great plan took shape in his mind. He would choose one special person from each land in the Kingdom. He would send them on missions to help children learn some of life's most important lessons. By helping the children, they would also learn a lot themselves.

Can you guess who he picked for the missions? Heada, Heartly and Doofer! They were the very best at thinking, feeling and doing.

To help them, The Great Theysayer gave each a gift: a thick book called the Tome to Heada, a magic crystal to Heartly and an amazing bag to Doofer.

Heada's book was stuffed with all the things they would need to know for their missions. She always carried it in her kangaroo-like pouch.

When anyone held Heartly's crystal, it glowed different colors to show feelings—pink for happiness, gray for sadness, and so on through a whole rainbow of emotions.

And in Doofer's amazing bag could be found all kinds of wonderful and surprising things to help them on their way.

After receiving their gifts, Heada, Heartly and Doofer began their exciting adventures. This is the story of one adventure.

Library of Congress Catalog Number: 85-80292

ISBN:

0-934275-00-9

Published in the United States by Family Skills, Inc.

Manufactured in the United States of America

# The Land of Listening

Listening: *Getting & Giving Attention.*

Authors
J. Thomas Morse, M.A.
Betty Gouge, Ph.D.
Deanna Tate, Ph.D.
John Eickmeyer

Research and Editing
Mary Thrash, M.A.
Teri Gathings, M.S.
Linda Stanislao, B.S.

Illustrations
Cathie Bleck

Published by Family Skills, Inc., Dallas, Texas.
Distributed by Kampmann & Company, Inc., New York, New York.

*Family Skills, Inc. wishes to acknowledge and express our sincere thanks to the hundreds of children and parents who contributed to the research, design, development and testing of the KidSkills™ interpersonal skills series.*

*I*n the kingdom of The Great Theysayer, alarm bells were ringing and red lights were flashing, all on account of Amanda.

"Tsk! Tsk!" clucked The Great Theysayer as he paced the Hall of Harmoniousness and read the incoming reports:

"They say Amanda's in a dither!
They say Amanda's in a stew!
They say she hasn't learned how to listen!
They say she doesn't know what to do!"

The Great Theysayer stroked his silvery beard and squinted thoughtfully for a moment. Then he spoke again, and his voice had the ring of command. "Bring me Heada!" he shouted. "And Heartly! And Doofer! I have a new mission for them — a mission to help Amanda!"

Recess was over for Mrs. Turlington's class. The children crowded through the door to smells of chalkdust, papers and leftover lunches. Amanda plopped into her chair, hoping the science lesson would be interesting.

But before she knew it, her thoughts were drifting. A jar of glitter on the art shelf reminded her of a dress she'd seen in a shop window. It had been covered with flashing sequins and bright beads. Amanda wondered if she'd ever wear a dress so lovely. And as she sat dreaming, she heard a voice call, "Amanda?"

The voice seemed to come from far away.

"Amanda!" called Mrs. Turlington.

Amanda sat up straight in her chair and looked at the teacher who stared back from the front of the classroom.

"Yes, Ma'am?" Amanda replied.

"Do you know the answer?"

"Which answer?" Amanda asked.

"The answer to the question I just asked. Weren't you listening?"

Amanda looked down at her desktop and rolled her pencil in its little groove. "I guess not," she said softly.

The class snickered, but Mrs. Turlington silenced it with one of her "zinger" looks.

"You know, Amanda," she said, "you haven't been listening well lately. This must be the tenth time this week."

The teacher hesitated for a moment as she thought about what to do. Then she said, "Maybe your parents and I should have a talk. See me after class, please."

The awful words had been spoken: "Your parents and I!" All the children – especially Michael Turner – knew they meant hard labor after school, and no TV. Michael had found himself in similar hot water not long before and had been a prisoner of homework ever since.

Michael looked across the rows at Amanda and tried to give her an understanding look, but he couldn't quite catch her eye.

Amanda, of course, felt very gloomy. And the note the teacher gave her to take home didn't help. Just carrying it made the bright autumn afternoon seem dark and threatening as Amanda trudged down the sidewalk toward the yellow school bus.

"Hey, Amanda! Save me a seat!" someone called behind her. It was Michael.

"Okay," she replied with a weak smile, "but don't expect me to listen to you. I don't do that very well."

Michael laughed. "Yeah, I know what you mean. Neither do *I*." He eyed his schoolbooks and added, "Extra homework doesn't help much either."

Amanda groaned. "I *try* to pay attention! But there are so many other things to think about, my mind starts to wander."

"Excuse me? What did you say?" Michael joked as they climbed aboard the bus. "I was thinking about something else."

"You think you're kidding," Amanda grinned in spite of herself, "but I really *do* that, even with friends."

"Yes, but it's teachers you have to worry about," sighed Michael as they took their seats. And with that the smiles faded from their faces, and the pair fell silent as the bus wheezed and rumbled off.

When Amanda got home, her mother didn't say much about the note from school. She just hugged Amanda and told her not to worry.

But Amanda *did* worry all that afternoon and evening. She worried through dinner and homework. She worried while watching TV. She worried as she brushed her teeth, put on her pajamas and laid out the next day's school clothes.

She worried as she climbed into bed and snuggled beneath the covers. And with worries spinning in her head, she fell into a restless slumber.

In her sleep, Amanda heard voices. At first she thought she was dreaming. But then she opened her eyes and saw three funny little characters standing beside her bed. How strange they looked!

Amanda blinked hard and rubbed her eyes. When she opened them again, the three little figures were still there.

"Who are you?" she asked in amazement.

At the sound of her voice, the three huddled together in the middle of the room. Then one stepped forward. She wore green glasses and carried a thick book in a pouch on her tummy like a kangaroo's. She looked very intelligent.

"We bring ratiocination to resolve your consternation," she said.

"What?" gasped Amanda.

"In other words," said the one with big floppy ears, "we'll help you learn to listen!" He hummed a little tune to himself, and his cuddly fur changed colors four times in as many seconds. Finally, it settled on a soft violet.

Meanwhile, the third little fellow was marching with a clatter back and forth across the floor like a wind-up toy, arms pumping up and down. He carried a big bag that bulged with stuff. And he seemed eager for action.

"BUZZZZZ-WHIRRRRR," he said. "Let's get going!"

"But who are you?" Amanda asked again.

"I'm Doofer," he said. "That's Heada. And *this,*" he indicated with a gesture at the furry fellow, "is Heartly."

"The crystal!" Heartly suddenly exclaimed and brought out a shining object. It looked like a huge diamond!

Amanda's eyes grew big at the dazzling sight. She reached out to take the glittering stone that Heartly held toward her. But when she did, it glowed a dull brown.

"Worried," said Heartly, taking back the crystal and shaking his head sadly. "Very worried."

"DING! DONG! Time to go, everybody!" crowed Doofer with a glance at one of the two watches he wore.

"Go? Where? How?" asked Amanda, reaching for her clothes.

"I'll do a door!" exclaimed Doofer. And pulling a big, blue pencil from his bag, he drew the outline of a door about three feet high on the wall of the bedroom. Then he took a shiny brass doorknob from the bag, popped it into place and gave it a twist. The door opened!

Away went the little threesome through the door with Amanda scrambling after them. She had to stoop to go through the low opening. But then she found herself in a strange, dimly lit passageway where she could walk upright.

"Wait for me!" she called. And hurrying along, she caught up just as they turned a corner.

The twisting, turning passage was like a cave or underground tunnel. Amanda felt excited and scared as the shadows gathered around them. There was a musty smell, like a cellar. And the rocky walls felt slippery with moisture. As their eyes adjusted to the darkness, they discovered that the dim light was coming from twinkling, blue-colored crystals sprinkled along the tunnel walls.

Sometimes they seemed lost. But then Heartly would wave his big ears and say: "Day and night, feels good to the right." Or Heada would think for a moment and announce, "This must be the way!" Or

Doofer would take a compass from his bag and check it for directions.

"But where are we going?" Amanda kept asking.

"On! Ahead! Forward! ... CLACK! CLACK! CLACK!" was the best answer she ever got.

After they had walked for some time, who should they meet but Michael coming from the opposite direction and looking very lost!

"Is that really you, Michael?" Amanda laughed. "How did you get here?"

Michael scratched his head. "I have no idea! How did you?"

"You wouldn't believe it if I told you," answered Amanda.

Excitedly, Amanda introduced Heada, Heartly and Doofer to Michael. The boy's eyes widened with astonishment as each little figure stepped forward. With that, they all went on together. They seemed to wander for a long, long time.

At last the tunnel widened a bit. At a bend in the passage, they came to a richly carved wooden door. In the center of the door was a golden ear about six inches high. Beneath it in beautifully painted gold letters was one word: ASK.

"What do we ask?" Michael wondered aloud. Nothing happened.

The ear was too high up for either Amanda or Michael to reach, and the group seemed stumped. Heartly was feeling puzzled and Heada was deep in thought, when Doofer began to buzz and shake.

"S-S-S-S-S-S-S-NICKETY POP!" he said. "I'll do stairs!" And so saying, he reached into his amazing bag and pulled out a strange looking contraption with a crank on one side. When he turned the crank, the contraption unfolded into a flight of stairs that extended up, up, up toward the ear on the door. "C'mon!" he yelled and beckoned Amanda to go up, which she quickly did.

"Hello?" she said into the ear. Still nothing happened.

"An intriguing problem," said Heada. "Hmmmmmm. Doors. Doors. Let me see. I know! We'll consult the Tome!"

The Tome seemed to be the big book she carried in her pouch, because in another moment Heada was flipping rapidly through its pages. "Here we are: Doors. It says we should request entry!"

"In other words … CLICK-ITY CLICK-ITY … we should ask to come in," said Doofer.

"Can we come in?" Amanda asked. The door clicked its lock and swung open.

Sweet, soft music floated from the other side of the door. "Oh, I love music!" squealed Heartly, his ears perking up. "Let's go!"

They all slipped through the open door and found themselves in a large chamber like the throne room of a castle. Amanda could hardly believe her eyes! On the walls around her were magnificent tapestries with pictures of musical instruments and singing birds and swinging bells and all sorts of things that made lovely sounds. Between the tapestries were antique ear trumpets, doctors' stethoscopes, megaphones, old fashioned radios, phonographs and other things used for listening.

To one side of the room were double doors opening out onto a garden, bright with sunshine and flowers. And toward the back of the chamber was a small platform where sat a woman in a high-backed chair. She was dressed in royal fashion, and in her hand she held a slim wand with a gold ear on top.

Seeing Amanda and her group, the woman turned and spoke into the gold ear.

"Hello!" Her voice boomed out as though from a loudspeaker. "Welcome to the Land of Listening!"

"E-e-excuse me?" Amanda stammered.

"The Land of Listening," repeated the woman in the same loud voice, "where you can learn to be better listeners."

"Oh, we just came in to hear the music," replied Michael. The music grew softer, then stopped.

The woman got up and came toward them. When she spoke again, it was in a normal tone.

"Just hearing isn't listening," she said with a smile.

Up close, Amanda could see the woman's dress was glittering with jewels and gold threads. The girl caught her breath and stared at the twinkling gems. She couldn't take her eyes off them, and neither could her friends.

"Wow!" Michael breathed.

"Have you ever seen a unicorn?" the woman suddenly asked, looking toward the garden.

"No," the children replied absently, their eyes fixed on the dress. They wondered how much it was worth. It must have cost millions and millions!

"If you do, your wishes come true — so they say," the woman went on. "But you've just missed this one."

"What?!" Amanda and Michael squeaked together. Looking up they saw that the woman was gazing toward the open double doors. Instantly they looked in the same direction, but all they saw was the gleaming tip of a white horn withdrawing out of sight.

"Run after it!" yelled Doofer. But by the time they all reached the doors, the unicorn was nowhere to be seen.

"I'll never see another!" moped Heartly as they plodded back across the room.

"Alas," said the woman kindly, "you heard but didn't *listen*." She sighed and shook her head the way Mrs. Turlington always did when the class wasn't paying attention, but her eyes twinkled a bit, too. Then she waved her wand and said, "My name is Queen Auricle. I'm Queen of Good Listeners. Who are you?"

"I'm Amanda," the girl replied. "This is my friend Michael. And this is Heada, Heartly and Doofer. They led us here."

"Yes, I know," said the Queen. "They followed The Great Theysayer's instructions. And now that you're here, how would you all like to become my subjects?"

"What do we have to do?" Amanda asked.

"Simply learn my rules for giving and getting attention — rules every good listener follows."

"Are they hard to learn?" Michael asked.

Queen Auricle smiled. "You'll be done before you know it."

Amanda looked at Michael who shrugged as if to say, "Why not?"

"All right," said Amanda. "What do we do first?"

First the Queen had them all sit in a circle, close their eyes and have a conversation with each other. With their eyes closed, they began to misunderstand each other's words.

"I like the Queen," Amanda said.

"You like the  bean !" Michael exclaimed. "What bean?"

"Seen what?" asked Heartly. "I can't see anything? My eyes are shut!"

"NUT! Who's a nut?" objected Heada.

"PUTT-PUTT-PUTT," clattered Doofer, as they all laughed.

"You see how important it is to listen with both your eyes and ears," said the Queen.

"If I'd been looking at your face instead of your dress," Amanda mused aloud, opening her eyes, "I wouldn't have missed the unicorn!"

"Now you're learning," the Queen said. "It's so easy to be distracted! But using your eyes and watching closely helps you pay attention."

"But sometimes I don't even realize that someone is talking to me," said Michael. "And even when I do, sometimes I don't *want* to listen."

"Very good, Michael!" cried the Queen, clapping her hands delightedly. "Those are two important things I want to talk about!"

Michael beamed, rather pleased with himself.

"The first step to being a good listener," the Queen continued, "is to let the person speaking to you know that you've heard. Then decide whether or not you can listen right then. If not, say so in a friendly way and suggest another time to talk. If you *can* listen, tell the person how much time you have. Next, set everything else aside. Turn off the TV or put down your toys. Then get comfortable and start using your eyes and ears for all they're worth!"

The Queen's words seemed to cast a spell over the group. They watched her closely with complete attention as she went on in her soft, musical voice.

"Watch the speaker's face and eyes. Pay attention to his or her expressions and tone of voice. They tell you so much. And by watching carefully, you let the person speaking know that you are really interested."

By now, everyone had gathered in a circle around the Queen. It was easy to see that *they* were really interested in what she was saying. They watched her so closely, they hardly blinked. The Queen looked at their wide-eyed faces and nodded approvingly. "Yes," she almost whispered, "yes, I can see you truly understand."

*thought, thought, thought*
*thought, thought, thought*
*thought, thought, thought*
*thought, thought, thought*
*thought, thought, thought*
*thought, thought, thought*
*thought, thought, thought*
*thought, thought, thought*
*thought, thought, thought*
*thought, thought, thought*
*thought, thought, thought*
*thought, thought, thought*

Suddenly, she clapped her hands, which seemed to break the spell that had fallen over the circle. "Now!" she said brightly, "Who knows how many words a minute a person can understand?"

Heada was ready with her thick book. "I have it here," she said as she flipped the pages of the Tome. "According to my source, the average human being understands up to 600 words per minute!"

"Excellent!" praised the Queen. "Now, how many words per minute can someone say?"

"ZZZZZZZZZZZINGO!" buzzed Doofer, extending a tape measure in front of Michael's mouth. "About 160," he reported.

"Very good!" said the Queen. "The difference between 600 and 160 is 440 words. That means you can think much faster than anyone can talk. So while you're listening, you're also thinking.

"But sometimes your thoughts are so interesting, you pay more attention to them than to what you're hearing. You stop really listening and use those 440 spare words to think about jewels or dresses or even what you're going to say next! Go ahead! Try it yourselves!"

"How?" everyone asked.

"Maybe Heada will read something to us," suggested the Queen, pointing to Heada's book. "See how much you think about while she's speaking."

So for the next few minutes, Heada read a passage from the Tome. It was all about humpback whales and the strange songs they sing to communicate with each other. Heartly tried hard to listen. But at the same time, he was also making up a rhyme in his head.

When Heada finished, the Queen turned to Heartly and said, "Tell us what you thought about while you were listening."

talk, talk, talk, talk
talk, talk, talk, talk
talk, talk, talk, talk

"I made up a whole rhyme," said Heartly proudly.

"Wonderful!" said the Queen. "May we hear it?"

So Heartly stood up and recited in his singsong little voice:

*"Plenty of words and plenty of time,*
*To wonder or daydream or make up a rhyme.*
*With all of those extras, there's no need to hurry.*
*You could use them to hope. Or use them to worry.*
*You could think up a song no one ever has heard.*
*Before you'd run out of so many spare words."*

"No wonder it's so hard to listen," said Amanda.

"Exactly!" remarked the Queen. Then turning to Heartly she said, "You did that so well! Tell us more."

Heartly beamed, and the crystal in his hand glowed a whole rainbow of colors. Then he began again as the Queen waved her wand gently over him.

*"You must be sure to*
*follow this rule:*
*Be ready to listen —*
*especially in school!*
*It works for you the other way, too,*
*When you want somebody to listen to you.*
*First, see if they're ready, then move*
*close by.*
*(It helps if you look them right straight*
*in the eye.)*
*Then cheerfully call out that person's name.*
*They'll be sure to listen, and you'll*
*do the same!"*

"Do you know what everyone's favorite sound is?" the Queen asked when Heartly had finished.

"One moment!" cried Heada as she hurriedly leafed through the Tome. "Here it is! The sound of his or her own name!"

"Correct!" laughed the Queen. "No one can resist it! Right, *Michael?*"

"Er...yes!" said Michael, rather flustered, for he had stopped listening to wonder how it would feel to touch the gold ear on Queen Auricle's wand.

"And once you have someone's attention," the Queen continued, "you should tell him or her what you want to talk about and how much time you need. If the person agrees, go ahead! Otherwise, try to set another time to get together."

"Finally," said the Queen, "talk; you have a listener. Remember to stop other activities while you're talking. All of us are like Doofer, Heada and Heartly. When we *do* other things or *think* other thoughts or *feel* other feelings while we're trying to talk or listen, it keeps us from communicating. When you finish speaking, thank your listener for listening."

"But Queen Auricle," Amanda asked, "how will we remember all you've taught us?"

Instantly, Doofer began rummaging in his bag and came up with a pencil and paper. "KA-BANGO!" he said. "I'll do a list so you won't forget."

"An excellent idea," said the Queen. "But remember: listening well is difficult. It takes practice, like any other skill. So work at it. And if you start to slip, I'll whisper a reminder." She picked up her wand and spoke one word softly into the gold ear: "Listen!" But Amanda and Michael heard the whisper as though the Queen had spoken into their own ears.

The children smiled with delight as Doofer began writing down the rules. Just as he was finishing, Queen Auricle spoke again.

"Amanda! Michael!"

They heard a new tone in the voice and both looked up quickly. The Queen was gazing steadily toward the open doors. "Have you ever seen a unicorn?" she asked.

Everyone looked, and there in the garden with his head just inside the double doors was a beautiful white unicorn! His mane was like silk, and the horn on his forehead gleamed like polished ivory. Then he was gone, but they had seen him for sure.

"I'm so happy," Heartly crowed, "I could jump for joy!"

"Fantastic!" breathed Heada. "I imagined they were only imaginary!"

"Clippity-clop! Clippity-clop!" clattered Doofer as he galloped around the room like a little unicorn.

"Amanda and Michael get a wish," laughed Queen Auricle happily. "What will it be?"

Amanda thought for only a moment. "I wish we could remember all we've learned when we go home," she said as she tucked her list of rules into a pocket of her jeans. Michael nodded in agreement.

"Wish granted," said the Queen. "And speaking of home, it's time to go. You both have school tomorrow."

With this, Queen Auricle touched the children's heads gently with the wand and said, "Thank you for listening. You will both be good listeners."

Suddenly, they were floating among pink clouds that swirled gently around them. The last thing they saw was Heada, Heartly and Doofer waving good-bye.

Before Amanda knew what could possibly happen next, she was waking up in her own bed with the pink dawn breaking outside her window.

Amanda felt wonderfully rested after her long sleep. As she dressed, she remembered that something had been troubling her the night before, but for a moment, she couldn't think what it was. Then it struck her: the problem at school and Mrs. Turlington's note!

She shuddered, preparing to feel miserable again, but she didn't. Something had changed. Something was different.

Much to her surprise, Amanda set off for school eagerly. She looked for Michael on the bus, and there he was with an empty seat beside him.

"I dreamed about you," they both said together as Amanda sat down.

Michael laughed. "What was yours?" he asked.

"Oh, a silly sort of dream," replied Amanda, embarrassed.

"Mine, too," said Michael.

There didn't seem to be anything more to say. So they sat quietly watching dark, wintry clouds gather in the sky beyond the windows of the bus.

"We're going to do a written exercise today," Mrs. Turlington said that morning, "and you'll have to listen carefully."

Amanda felt the slightest hint of worry at these words. But then she remembered her new confidence.

"I want you to write down the sentences I'm going to read," Mrs. Turlington continued, "and punctuate them properly according to the tone of my voice and the expression of my face. Does everyone understand?"

There was a murmur of agreement from the class. Then someone called out: "Look! It's snowing!"

All eyes turned toward the windows, but Mrs. Turlington's didn't linger there long. "Class," she said, "we have all seen snow before, so let's get back to work."

"But it's the first snow this year," protested a voice.

"And I hope you all enjoy it *after* school," the teacher said. "Now if everyone is ready, we'll begin."

All the sentences were tough. While she was listening to them, Amanda longed to glance out at the magically falling snow the way the other children were doing. She wanted to think about snow and snowmen and snowball fights. But a familiar, whispery voice in her ear seemed to say, "Listen!" So she looked hard for exclamation points in Mrs. Turlington's eyes and listened for question marks in her voice.

When the exercise was over, Amanda sighed with relief. Mrs. Turlington graded the papers at her desk while the class did a reading assignment. A low hum of study settled over the room, broken at times by little yelps of joy as the snow fell more and more heavily outside.

"Amanda!"

Amanda looked up to see Mrs. Turlington beaming at her.

"Amanda, this is excellent! You got a hundred  percent!"

Amanda's eyes opened wide with surprise.

"And so did Michael!" Mrs. Turlington said. "Perhaps you'll both tell us how you did it."

Amanda and Michael felt the eyes of the whole class upon them. What could they say? They couldn't tell everyone about Queen Auricle and Heartly and Heada and Doofer. No one would believe it. So Amanda

said, "First, decide that you want to listen and remove all distractions."

"Then get comfortable and ready to listen," piped up Michael.

"And watch the speaker's eyes," they both said together.

And in this way, Amanda and Michael shared all the remarkable things they suddenly knew about good listening — about how to give and get attention. The class was amazed. And Mrs. Turlington was wonderstruck!

After school, Michael walked home from the bus stop with Amanda through the deepening snow. They didn't say much as they walked. They both seemed to be thinking. Then Michael stood still.

"In my dream," he said in a hushed voice, "you put a note in your pocket."

Amanda didn't say a word. Silently she reached into her pocket and pulled out a folded piece of paper. Both Amanda and Michael caught their breaths as she unfolded it to find the listening rules written in Doofer's funny, blocky letters.

There in the lower right hand corner were also three little signatures: "Heada, Heartly and Doofer."

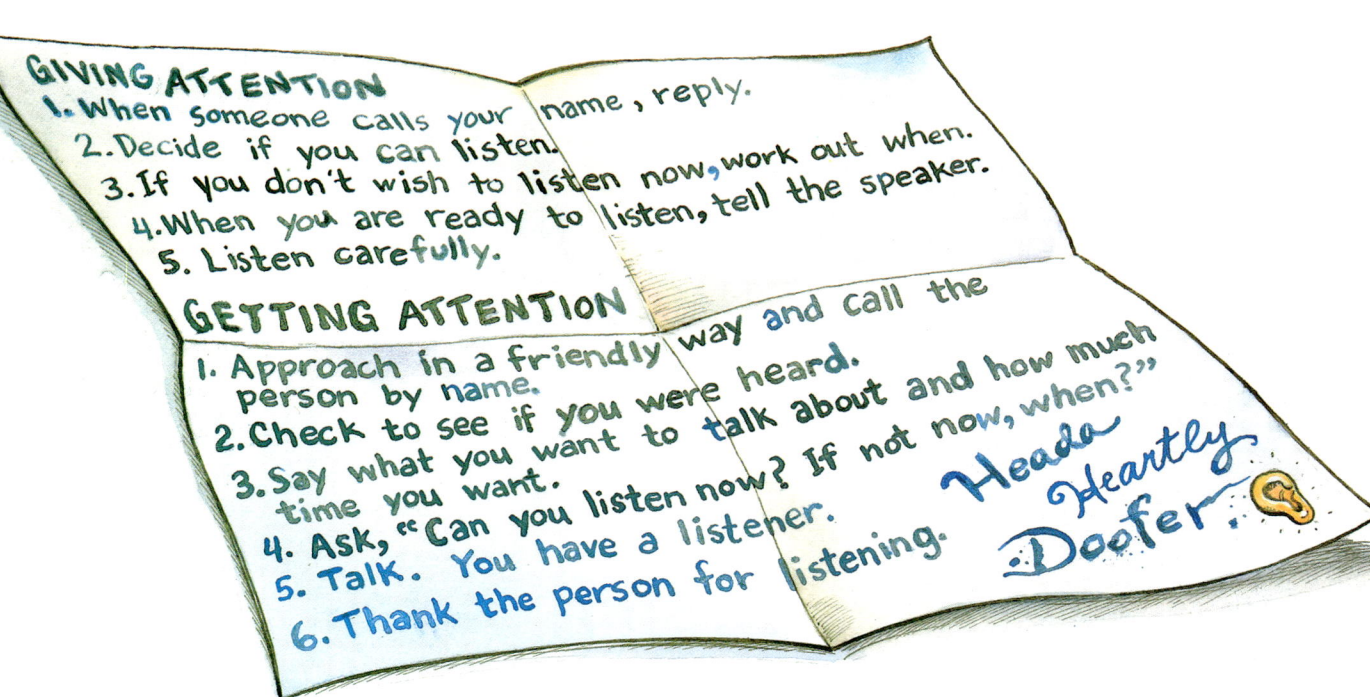

GIVING ATTENTION
1. When someone calls your name, reply.
2. Decide if you can listen.
3. If you don't wish to listen now, work out when.
4. When you are ready to listen, tell the speaker.
5. Listen carefully.

GETTING ATTENTION
1. Approach in a friendly way and call the person by name.
2. Check to see if you were heard.
3. Say what you want to talk about and how much time you want.
4. Ask, "Can you listen now? If not now, when?"
5. Talk. You have a listener.
6. Thank the person for listening.

Heada Heartly Doofer.

For a moment, they just stared. Then they began to laugh. And laughing still, they raced away to play in the falling snow.

But they didn't make a snowman.

They made a white unicorn.

*T*hey say you did well!" said The Great
Theysayer. "Amanda and Michael learned to
listen. And all of you worked together."
Little Heartly could barely contain his joy at
hearing such praise, and he danced a jig on the marble
floor of the Hall of Harmoniousness, big ears
flapping as he sang:

"Are we finished?
Are we through?
Is that all
There is to do?"

The Great Theysayer's eyes twinkled.
"Yes, for now," he said. "This mission is complete.
But there is much more to be done. And many more
children to visit and help. Many more. Many more."

And still repeating "Many more" over and over to
himself, The Great Theysayer paced majestically out
of the Hall.

The three watched him go.

"Our task is not yet accomplished, it seems," said
Heada thoughtfully. "More adventures yet to come.
That is reasonable. Quite correct. Indisputable."

Suddenly, Doofer began to spin rapidly around
like a whirlygig.

"Sometimes," he said, making a sound like a
kettle about to boil, "you *are* unreasonably reasonable!
S-S-S-S-NICKETY POP! KA-BANG!"

# Heada's Dictionary
## Words from the Tome

Astonishment — *amazement or wonder*

Auricle — *outside part of the ear*

Consternation — *fear or worry that makes you feel helpless*

Contraption — *a complicated machine*

Distractions — *something that causes confusion*

Flustered — *confused, nervous*

Harmoniousness — *feelings, ideas, interests combined pleasantly*

Indisputable — *something that cannot be questioned*

Intriguing — *interesting or curious*

Magnificent — *beautiful, grand, stately*

Miserable — *very sad*

Ratiocination — *to reason using logic*

Tapestries — *heavy cloth that has designs*

Unreasonably reasonable — *unusually sensible or wise*

Wheezed — *breathed hard and loudly*

# Other books from Family Skills:

## School Age:

Self-Esteem: *Being a Friend to Myself*
Cooperation: *Working Together*
Feelings: *Dealing With Feelings*
Responsibility: *Making and Carrying Out a Plan*
Self-Talk: *Thinking and Feeling Good When Things Go Wrong*
Friendship: *Making Friends*
Friendship: *Keeping Friends*

## Preschool:

Self-Esteem: *Adjusting to New Experience*
Responsibility: *Making and Living With Choices*
Feelings: *Experiencing Feelings*
Responsibility: *Understanding and Accepting Limits*
Self-Esteem: *Accepting and Knowing Myself*
Friendship: *Sharing and Taking Turns*